Brown

ESSENTIAL **DK** MANAGERS

LONDON, NEW YORK, MUNICH,
MELBOURNE, AND DELHI

DK LONDON

Project Editor Nicky Munro
DTP Designer Rajen Shah
Production Controller Kevin Ward
Managing Editor Adèle Hayward
Managing Art Editor Karen Self
Category Publisher Stephanie Jackson

DK DELHI

Project Editor Sheema Mookherjee
Editor Rimli Borooah
Project Art Editor Kavita Dutta
DTP Designer Balwant Singh
Managing Editor Ira Pande
Managing Art Editor Aparna Sharma
Editorial Consultant Anita Roy

First published in Great Britain in 2003
by Dorling Kindersley Limited, 80 Strand
London WC2R 0RL

A Penguin Company
2 4 6 8 10 9 7 5 3 1

A CIP catalogue record for this book is
available from the British Library

ISBN 1 4053 0027 2

Reproduced by Colourscan, Singapore
Printed and bound in Hong Kong
by Wing King Tong

See our complete catalogue at
www.dk.com

CONTENTS

INTRODUCTION

Your relationship with your boss is one of the most important factors in achieving a successful career. Understanding how your boss thinks and works is the key to building a productive partnership. Managing Your Boss explains how you can get the best out of your boss, whether you are working under pressure or on routine tasks. It shows you how to assess the type of boss you have, suggests how to meet the challenges of working with a difficult boss, and teaches you how to play to your boss's strengths and weaknesses. Practical advice is given to help you define your goals and pursue self-development. A self-assessment questionnaire evaluates how well you manage your boss. Packed with 101 tips, this book will help you turn your boss into your greatest advocate.

ASSESSING YOUR SITUATION

You can only be effective in your job if you learn to manage your boss. Assess what you want in your career and what you need from your boss so that you can work jointly to reach your goals.

FORMING AN ALLIANCE

You and your boss need each other to succeed, and your relationship is of vital importance. Learn from, and manage this useful ally, so that you can work together effectively as a team, gain job satisfaction, and achieve your career aims.

1	Think of your boss as a key customer and your best advocate.

2	Assess what you and your boss need to work on to be a team that achieves results.

MANAGING YOUR FUTURE

You are responsible for your career development and for being effective in your current job. Your boss and others can help you, but ultimately you manage your own future. Learn to manage your relationship with your boss and remember that she is only human and may need some help. Assess your own and your boss's strengths and weaknesses and note down areas that need development. Although your boss may not be ideal, make the best of what is likely to be a transitional situation. If you have a good boss, take full advantage of the period during which you are working together.

ASPIRING FOR THE TOP ▼

In a flat organizational hierarchy, which has few management layers, you need to stand out as exceptionally competent to gain promotion. In an organization with just three hierarchical layers, there will be intense competition among peers in the lower layers.

■ *1 person*   ■ *15 people*   ☐ *300 people*

LEARNING FROM YOUR BOSS

If you succeed, your boss has a greater chance of success. If your boss is successful, you will be seen as part of a winning team. Bosses like to be known for producing winners. An experienced boss can teach you good judgment in different situations. The contacts that your boss has made can be very useful to you in your career. Be clear to your boss about what help you need to excel at your job, and do not be too proud to take it.

3 Acquire your boss's skills by observation.

▼ GAINING KNOWLEDGE

Your boss probably has wider and more depth of experience than you. Learn from your boss – encourage her to pass on to you job knowledge and understanding of how the organization works.

ASSESSING YOURSELF

When you and your boss share important values and goals, you are more likely to succeed in your job. Understand yourself and what you want out of life and your career, and then ask your boss for help in working towards those goals.

4 Match your goals – professional and personal – to your values.

5 Write down your aspirations in order of their importance to you.

DETERMINING VALUES

Be clear about the values that are important to you and decide which career or organization will be compatible with them. Your boss can understand your motivation only if you know what your priorities are. Think about what is important to you and listen to your feelings. Talk to family and friends about what you would like to achieve and where your uncertainties lie. As you explain, listen carefully to your own choice of words. They can reveal what you really feel about your stated aims.

DETERMINING YOUR VALUES AND GOALS

VALUES	GOALS
BUILDING WEALTH	Accumulate assets of £500,000 within 10 years.
CAREER ADVANCEMENT	Gain recognition as an expert in my field within five years.
HEALTHY LIFESTYLE	Have a balanced diet and exercise regularly.
SECURITY	Pay off all my debts within two years.
QUALITY TIME WITH FAMILY	Ensure all weekends off and five weeks holiday per year.
SPIRITUAL RENEWAL	Set aside 15 minutes daily to meditate.

SETTING YOUR GOALS

Being sure about your goals will help you to discuss with your boss, when the time comes, what you want from your career and how he can help you to achieve your aims. Make a comprehensive list of goals in all the areas of your life – for example, in work, learning, or relationships – because each one affects your personal work-life balance and the extent to which you can expect your boss's help.

6 Think of goals associated with your mind, body, heart, and spirit.

▼ **VISUALIZING GOALS**
Close your eyes and think of your goals – a prestigious job, wealth, family. Imagine you have achieved them. Are you happy and are these the right goals? Note what you have learned by looking at your future.

MAKING CHOICES

By visualizing the future, you will identify a number of goals. If you have too many different goals, you will need to prioritize them. Some may be incompatible with others, or with your view of life. Once you are clear about what is important to you, you may set upon a different path in your job or change careers altogether.

◄ **ANALYZING YOUR OPTIONS**
On a sheet of paper, list your goals on the left, and create columns for different career options. Give a score out of 10 against each goal. Add up each column to choose the best career.

Goals	A	B	C
Minimum salary £65,000 per annum plus bonus	8	6	3
Career development potential	7	9	4
Interesting and challenging job	5	8	7
Commuting to work less than 30 minutes per day	2	5	9
Opportunity to gain further qualifications	8	8	5
Build on my sector experience	6	8	7
TOTAL	36	44	35

Key to Career Options: A : Global Enterprises Inc.
B : National Organization Plc.
C : Local Company Ltd.
Score out of 10 indicates B is nearest to ideal

9

ASSESSING YOUR BOSS TYPE

Throughout your career you are likely to work for different bosses. Assess which of the following bosses – ideal and less than ideal – most closely match your boss's style, in order to understand effective techniques for managing your type of boss.

7 Change the way you manage your boss according to his or her type.

8 Gain respect from your colleagues by pleasing the perfectionist boss.

THE IDEAL BOSS

Draw up a specification of the ideal boss and review your own situation. If your current boss does not measure up to your ideal, you can identify areas for development. A successful boss has a clear vision of where he and his organization are going, and is interesting and inspiring to work with. He sets high standards for himself as well as for others. His organization skills are excellent, and he delegates effectively by motivating his team to work well. The ideal boss is self-confident and supportive of his team. He is aware of the need to give praise and recognition to others. Before your next career move, assess at the interview how well your potential boss meets these criteria and select a job with the nearest to ideal boss.

▼ **GAINING YOUR COMMITMENT**

A good boss encourages in you a sense of responsibility for ongoing work, and develops your ability to manage yourself and take ownership of projects. This style leads to greater commitment from you than if your boss just tells you what to do.

YOUR BOSS'S STYLE

Instructing	Persuading	Sharing	Involving	Empowering

THE PERFECTIONIST BOSS

A perfectionist takes high standards to the extreme and is difficult to please. She is reluctant to delegate in case you fall short of all-round excellence, and is likely to spot anything wrong, from a typing error to non-compliance with procedures. This boss works best in an ordered environment with few interruptions. Recognize her need to feel in control and valued for her expertise by giving frequent progress reports.

9 Advise your boss of any problem as early as possible.

QUESTIONS TO ASK YOURSELF

Q Does my boss communicate effectively with the team as well as outsiders?

Q Does my boss have a good track record at his current and previous jobs?

Q Does my boss make team members feel a sense of responsibility for ongoing projects?

Q Does my boss inspire me to feel a greater sense of commitment towards my work?

THE CHAOTIC BOSS

This boss is often unfocused and moves from one idea to the next instead of following one through. His in-tray is left unattended and his tasks are not delegated. However, he is usually enthusiastic about people and knowledge and can be helpful and informative. Utilize these strengths while you reduce his workload. Leave him with minimal paperwork and meet him briefly every day to plan and decide the crucial tasks to be delegated to you.

▼ UNDERSTANDING GENDER

Although it would be wrong to assess particular managers by generalizing about typical female and male traits, there are broad patterns that are characteristic of each gender.

FEMALE BOSS | MALE BOSS

Has well-developed language ability

Is able to interpret visual data well

Solves problems by talking them through

May withdraw to solve a problem

Opts for mediation and not confrontation

Has quick outbursts and forgets them fast

THE INTERFERING BOSS

A boss who interferes cannot resist checking on the progress of delegated tasks and will hover around your desk. This boss is afraid that if things go wrong, you will not tell him until it is too late. Keeping him regularly updated may not be enough. Difficult as it may seem, ask him to look closely at your work, approach, and progress. He should see that you get on with your work competently and efficiently without his constant input, and will realize that such tight control is unnecessary.

Team member keeps boss regularly informed on progress

Boss assigns project to team member

Boss asks team member for feedback on project frequently, but does not receive regular updates

▲ HANDLING INTERFERENCE
With an interfering boss, you will be closely supervised – learn not to be irritated by it. Indulge your boss's need to know every aspect of ongoing projects and eventually he will be convinced that you can be trusted.

10 Win over the trust of the interfering boss.

THE ABSENTEE BOSS

A boss who never seems to be there when you need her moves quickly from one task to another, enjoys trouble-shooting, and is always disappearing to sort out a crisis. She assimilates information quickly and expects others to do the same. This boss expects you to use your initiative and thinks she has given adequate direction. Build relationships with others who work closely with her to obtain information that she has not been around to supply. Ask your boss for her guidance and support to help you carry out delegated tasks. Learn to give short, focused updates, and be persistent in striving for two-way communication.

Boss trusts employee and allows him to work without constant interference

Boss observes that employee is successfully carrying out tasks on his own

THE AGGRESSIVE BOSS

If your boss has outbursts when under stress, learn to handle the aggression. He has plenty of energy and drive that can be channelled constructively. The aggressive boss is used to people agreeing with him, and is intimidating when faced with dissent. When this boss launches into a tirade, stand your ground firmly and suggest a meeting later to explain how you felt about his manner. Emphasize how important it is to you to prevent the recurrence of such an attack as it is demotivating and upsetting, and see if his behaviour can change.

Boss loses trust in team member and feels unable to delegate important work

DOS AND DON'TS

✔ Do check up on the staff turnover of a potential boss.

✔ Do praise decisions your boss makes.

✔ Do ask for a decision well before it is due if your boss takes a long time to decide.

✘ Don't ask a reluctant boss to make too many decisions.

✘ Don't suggest a meeting time without looking at your boss's schedule.

✘ Don't forget to find out how your boss likes to receive information.

THE RELUCTANT BOSS

A boss who is reluctant wants to be liked and is slow to make any decision that might cause conflict. You will receive plenty of praise but no negative feedback, however constructive. The most you can expect are general comments about your work. Ask her for feedback and show her that you react well. This boss avoids prioritizing and puts off decisions for fear of adverse results. Take the initiative and make decisions, with the basics agreed upon beforehand. You can gain autonomy and experience working with this type of boss.

 11 Agree on how much guidance you will need.

 12 Prompt the reluctant boss to make decisions.

RESPONDING TO YOUR BOSS

The ideal boss is assertive and easy to respond to in the same way. When you are faced with an aggressive or passive boss, assess your habitual response. You may choose to react in the same way or be more constructive and assertive than your boss.

13 Discuss matters with an aggressive boss only after the outburst is over.

Boss's angry outburst is excessive and relentless

Team member exclaims loudly to startle her into stopping

FACING AGGRESSION

A directly aggressive boss lets her anger out, perhaps by shouting at you if you make a mistake. Assess whether you can cope with this by mentally withdrawing each time it happens. Deal with the situation by maintaining eye contact, remaining calm, and waiting for her anger to subside. She may even apologize soon afterwards. If this does not work, point out that shouting is not helping either of you, and suggest that you talk through the problem in private when she is calmer.

◀ **STOPPING THE TIRADE**
If all else fails, you may have to resort to surprise tactics to halt your boss's tirade. Say her name loudly to interrupt her and give yourself a chance to speak.

RECOGNIZING INDIRECT AGGRESSION

An indirectly aggressive boss lets her anger out in subtle ways – for example, by making sarcastic comments, or being more resistant to your ideas than usual. She is taking the indirect route instead of confronting you. In the worst possible instance, you may hear rumours or overhear your boss complaining about your work. Assess your response quickly. Tackle the situation before it escalates further, especially if you find yourself being left out of important decisions. At a one-to-one meeting with your boss, discuss your feelings, ask questions to help you understand the problem, and propose a way forward.

HELPING A PASSIVE BOSS

A passive boss avoids confrontation and fails to tackle awkward situations. He appears calm but can be just as difficult to deal with as an aggressive boss. This kind of boss has an excessive desire to please his superiors and will procrastinate for fear of failure. Your response to him should be assertive and cooperative. Encourage him to meet with you to review progress – he will agree to this since he wants to appear helpful. Help him to voice his concerns by asking open questions assertively.

14 Use empathy to deal with a passive boss.

▼ **HANDLING PASSIVITY**
With a passive boss, you may need to use your own initiative to solve problems. Do this as tactfully as possible so that your boss does not mind you speaking up.

Boss is silent at a crucial stage of talks with client

Client is concerned at lack of progress

Team member makes suggestion and moves the discussion forward

THINGS TO DO

1. Think about how you can change your habitual response to your boss.

2. Ask for time to think about what your boss has said if you feel that you need to.

3. Anticipate a positive response from your boss and you may get it.

BEING MUTUALLY ASSERTIVE

The assertive boss has a realistic view of himself and others. He is easy to respond to assertively as he makes you feel you have a valued contribution to make. Aggressive or passive bosses ignore the rights of others to be listened to and to express their own opinions. An assertive boss listens to you with an open mind. If he disagrees, he does so in a constructive way, without attacking you verbally or manipulating your reply. You can behave assertively and say what you feel, even if you disagree, as you work together towards a solution.

MAKING THE MOST OF DELEGATION

A crucial management skill affecting your situation at work, delegation is the key to your boss's effective management of you. If your boss is a good manager, she will also be a good delegator, and together you will be a productive and efficient team.

15 Accept routine tasks, but minimize the time you spend on them.

16 Be enthusiastic about taking on responsibilities.

17 Negotiate realistic deadlines for new tasks.

TAKING THE CUE FROM YOUR BOSS

Your boss should have the professional skills needed at her level, and be committed to the development of her team members. Observing how your boss manages you and others will give you insights into the way you like or do not like to be managed. Managers ensure tasks are done through others, and it is important to assess your boss's delegating skills. Consider whether you have the opportunity to learn from her, and to use your newly acquired knowledge and skills.

REVIEWING ROLES ▶
The founder of a successful company was now a constraint on its growth. Open discussion with his team led him to trust his managers to work within clear lines of responsibility.

CASE STUDY
Angela Everett worked in a profitable niche business built on the charismatic founder's personal qualities. She had been brought in to structure the company for further growth. The new management team was finding it difficult to work effectively because Angela's boss insisted on making key customer decisions. Angela organized an externally facilitated session with the boss and the management team.

Together they reviewed goals and responsibilities, and debated the risks of devolving some of the key responsibilities the boss had retained. This honest review enabled the company to utilize the boss's undoubted personal charisma on PR and other high-profile activities. The management team made sure this was backed by effective customer service and operations. Turnover increased and within three years the company expanded threefold.

ASSESSING YOUR BOSS AS A DELEGATOR

Ask yourself these questions about your boss. If you answer mostly "no", you may need to manage your boss so that, over time, she understands that virtually everything – except strategy or elements of her role that concern leading her team – could be delegated to you.

" *Does my boss realize that being in control does not mean she has to make all the decisions?* "

" *Does she take the time to help me develop the skills I need to perform a delegated task well?* "

" *Is my boss secure enough not to be worried about her own position if I perform delegated tasks well?* "

" *Does my boss delegate the whole job to me, giving me full authority to make decisions?* "

ACCEPTING DELEGATION

You can influence how much work your boss delegates to you. Even if you suspect she only passes on the tasks that she least likes, you can manage her to become a better delegator. Encourage an unwilling delegator at first by accepting the most routine tasks. Make sure that you meet the deadlines and standards set by your boss. Give her feedback on your progress and ask if there is more work that you can take off her hands. As you prove that you are competent, your boss will entrust you with more and more responsible tasks.

Boss assigns task outside employee's job scope

Employee asks for additional training to do the job well

DELEGATING TOO MUCH ▶
Some bosses delegate all aspects of their job. While this may be a good chance to prove yourself, assess whether you have the required skills and time to perform these tasks.

18 Ensure that you are given authority along with additional responsibility.

REVIEWING YOUR CURRENT RELATIONSHIP

People who work together can fall into a fixed routine. As organizational goals move on and you develop, assess if your and your boss's behaviour patterns are still effective. If not, help your boss to accept that the current relationship needs to change.

19	Change yourself rather than expect your boss to change.

Draw up a list with two columns – Strengths and Development Areas

↓

Fill each column by imagining what your boss, or his colleagues and superiors, would write

↓

Review the list, reflecting on the insights from each different perspective

↓

Pick an area for improvement and discuss it with your boss, along with its expected gains

▲ **EXPLORING DIFFERENT PERSPECTIVES**
Look at how you and your boss work together from viewpoints other than your own. Collate the different perspectives and work systematically through each development area with your boss.

ASSESSING WHAT NEEDS TO CHANGE

Focus on the objectives that you and your boss are responsible for achieving in the organization. Review how you tackle these responsibilities together and identify when your relationship works well or not so well. Be specific about what you want to change. Ask questions about what helps and what hinders you and your boss at work and prepare practical suggestions, with benefits for both of you, to raise in discussion.

DOS AND DON'TS

✔ Dos	✘ Don'ts
Do expect to continuously improve in your job.	Don't act without anticipating what your boss might think.
Do seek to understand your boss's perspective.	Don't take your boss for granted.
Do look for a win-win solution for both you and your boss.	Don't resist change without considering the consequences fully.
Do review your existing relationship with your boss, especially if you feel nothing has changed for some time.	Don't forget to review with your boss what the two of you have learned through working together.

MOVING TOWARDS A WIN-WIN SOLUTION

After suggesting a change to your boss, listen to his response. If he does not agree with you, ask questions that entail more than just a yes or no answer, to understand his point of view. Discuss the benefits of your suggestion and be open to alternative proposals. Through a two-way discussion with both of you listening to each other, you can find a win-win solution. If your boss still does not see the need to change, it might be time to start looking for a new job.

20 Identify recurring situations that you can improve.

21 End all discussions with your boss on a positive note.

Bonus divided unequally between boss and employees

boss 70% employees 30%

Effective partnership brings the team more earnings and bonus. Split equally between boss and employees, both get more than before

boss 50% employees 50%

▲ WINNING AS A TEAM
An improvement in your working relationship with your boss will make you more effective as a team. Looking for a win-win solution will provide more gains than you could achieve on your own.

22 Give a new boss a fair chance to prove himself.

EXPECTING CHANGE

Some time in the future you or your boss will move on. Be prepared for a new relationship and assess your new boss objectively. If you had a good relationship with your previous boss or worked with him for a long time, it may be difficult to avoid comparing a new boss with the old one. To build a good rapport with your new boss, you will need to appreciate fresh ideas and avoid constantly referring to the past. Both of you will have to invest time to achieve an effective partnership.

WORKING WITH YOUR BOSS

Managing your boss begins with managing yourself, performing well, and using initiative. Understand what is important to your boss so that you can help him work well and receive help in return.

ANTICIPATING NEEDS

Show initiative, and save your boss time, by understanding how he works and anticipating his needs. When you brief your boss on a problem, present your solution at the same time. If your boss is part of the problem, try to give feedback constructively.

> **23** Think about what your boss needs to know and give frequent updates.

▲ SETTING UP MEETINGS
If your boss receives information best by listening, ensure that you have face-to-face meetings supplemented by phone calls.

KNOWING YOUR BOSS

It is crucial to know your boss's style of working and be clear how you will communicate with each other. Think about how he prefers to receive information and how frequently. Your boss may be happy with a series of quick meetings to address problems as the need arises. Or he may manage better with structured meetings, asking for an agenda in advance. Find out if your boss takes in facts best by listening, or prefers reading. Ask if he would like to hear a verbal presentation, followed by your report, or if he would prefer to read it first and then ask questions.

KEEPING YOUR BOSS INFORMED

By understanding what information your boss wants and how often he likes feedback, you can keep him up-to-date on important issues and be left alone to do your work. Ask him if he prefers you to give a summary of every aspect of a project, or to report only unexpected results. You may need to go for quick, frequent updates or periodic reviews according to the nature of the project. Your boss's need for information can change, so check whether his needs are being met.

> **24** Time your reports according to the project stage.

> **25** Submit reports if your boss prefers written records.

ASSESSING HOW TO COMMUNICATE WITH YOUR BOSS

MEDIUM	PURPOSE	WHEN USEFUL
E-MAIL 	To record communication, and for non-urgent queries	Your boss is happy to use e-mail and has time to deal with it. Use it when you need a record of your query or want your boss to note an achievement.
PHONE	To address issues promptly that can be dealt with verbally.	Your boss does not mind interruptions and copes well with quick verbal exchanges. Limit the interruptions by only phoning on important issues.
BRIEF AD-HOC MEETING	To discuss issues that have just arisen and need urgent attention.	Your boss is happy with quick face-to-face interruptions. Use it when your boss needs some important information or to resolve an urgent issue.
MEMO 	To explain why a document is being sent, or to act as a reminder.	Your boss corresponds by memo and prefers to sort an in-tray of papers rather than deal with e-mail. Use a memo if you need to make a point for the record.
FORMAL MEETING	To discuss issues face to face, following an agreed agenda.	Your boss responds well to planned one-to-one meetings. Use these regularly to keep your boss updated on progress and for coaching and two-way feedback.

Analyzing Problems

Problems, such as failing to meet deadlines or making ill-advised decisions, reflect poorly on your own and your boss's reputation. Understanding the causes of problems is the first step towards solving them. Collect all the facts about difficulties that recur in the work you and your boss do, or in your relationship, and review them to identify the cause. List all the possible solutions you can think of to tackle the problem. Assess the benefits of each solution from the point of view of your boss and that of the organization. The one with the most benefits is likely to be the best solution for you to present to your boss.

26 Ask yourself what you would change if you could wave a magic wand.

27 Summarize your solution on one sheet of paper for your boss.

Creating a Winning Proposal

Gather information about a recurring problem

↓

Identify when the problem occurs and its likely causes

↓

List your ideas for a solution to the problem

↓

Sum up the benefits and likely risks of the solution

↓

Complete the review by adding a plan of action

Questions to Ask Yourself

Q Do I make an effort to find out the causes of problems?

Q Have I gathered information about a recurring problem?

Q Have I identified when the problem occurs?

Q Have I thought about all possible solutions?

Q Am I well prepared to answer any query my boss might have?

Q Am I aware of the risks and benefits of my solution?

Presenting Solutions

Prepare a summary of your analysis of the problem, its impact, and likely causes to present to your boss. This will help a methodical boss to check the detail and the logic, especially if he likes to view matters one step at a time. The same summary works equally well for a boss who finds detail tedious, as it gives him an instant overview. Discuss with your boss what needs to be done by whom and by when, and jointly put together an action plan, including review dates, in order to present a complete solution.

RAISING ISSUES

If your boss's weaknesses and your inability to compensate for them are endangering your success as a team, you need to consider whether it is worth addressing the issue with your boss. A frank discussion may benefit you both and help to resolve problems before they become too difficult to handle. However, if you feel that he may react adversely and your job might be at stake, try to ignore the issues that you can live with and raise only those that are vital.

28 Uncover hidden conflicts with your boss before they get out of hand.

29 Raise issues only when your boss can give you full attention.

▼ CRITICIZING CONSTRUCTIVELY
Developmental feedback should be in the form of constructive suggestions rather than hard-hitting criticism.

GIVING FEEDBACK

The willingness of you and your boss to give each other constructive feedback is a measure of the effectiveness of your relationship. Your feedback can be motivational, in the form of praise, or developmental, which focuses on what you see as your boss's shortcomings. This is the hardest feedback to give, so think about what to say and how to phrase it constructively. Write down examples of his behaviour and the impact it has on you. Anticipate his reaction and decide whether the benefits of giving feedback outweigh the risks.

Employee suggests ways of improving the working partnership

Boss listens carefully to his well-considered points

POINTS TO REMEMBER

- You should gather facts and analyze the causes of a problem you are trying to resolve, before moving on to the solutions.
- Your solutions are more likely to be accepted if you present the benefits to all those affected.
- To be successful, feedback needs to be constructive.
- Praise for your colleagues and boss should be genuine and motivational.

PRESENTING YOURSELF POSITIVELY

P *resenting yourself and your work well will create a favourable impression with your boss. Always be positive in all your dealings with your boss – this in turn will help your boss to be upbeat and in the right frame of mind for success.*

30 Keep yourself fit to retain energy for work and achieve high productivity.

31 Adopt a good posture and hold your head high.

LOOKING GOOD ▼
Always appear well-prepared, keep eye contact, and communicate key points clearly. This will make your boss more receptive to the purpose of your presentation.

CREATING A GOOD IMPRESSION

Be aware of the image you project, both by your manner, and the clothes you wear. Positive body language will reassure your boss that you can do the job. Emulate the dress code of people at a level above you. In this way, you project to your boss, and others, the idea that you could fulfil a more senior position and that you have the authority and ambition to succeed. Present your written communications professionally to engender the same confidence in the work that you produce.

Employee presents ideas in a self-assured and professional manner

Boss is impressed with presentation and receptive to new ideas

DOING MORE THAN EXPECTED

Always under-promise and over-deliver rather than the other way round if you want to delight your boss. Doing more than is expected of you will get you noticed and persuade your boss that you are worth investing in for the future. It is reassuring for her to know that you complete work before the deadline and arrive on time for meetings. Be the first to come up with innovative solutions and be a cooperative team member. Keep asking yourself: What else would help my boss?

32 Always think about the consequences of your actions for others.

▼ INFLUENCING OTHERS

Through a positive approach, you convey that you are part of a successful team, in turn affecting the attitude of others.

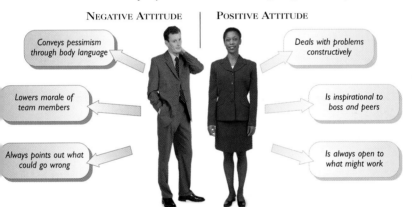

NEGATIVE ATTITUDE | POSITIVE ATTITUDE

Conveys pessimism through body language

Lowers morale of team members

Always points out what could go wrong

Deals with problems constructively

Is inspirational to boss and peers

Is always open to what might work

MANAGING MOODS

Your physical expressions can affect your psychological state. Simply smiling will make you feel better. Manage your mood by reflecting on past successes. Help others, including your boss, to value their achievements and feel good about themselves.

FEELING POSITIVE

Your boss will want to be around people who give energy rather than drain it. If you are always constructive in your approach, you can renew your boss's energy when work is particularly challenging. Both your roles as leaders, at different levels, involve being inspirational to others. You can maintain morale and motivate the team to achieve objectives by being positive. When stating an objective, let your boss and peers know what you can do rather than what you cannot.

DEFINING BOUNDARIES

You and your boss share the responsibility of developing a successful working relationship. Building good rapport, and defining and understanding the boundaries of each other's roles are the first steps towards an effective partnership.

33 Agree on the boundaries with your boss early in the relationship.

34 Align your aims with those that are most important to your boss.

▼ CLARIFYING
WORK CRITERIA
Seek your boss's help when setting your objectives and ask him to outline the criteria on which the standard of your work will be judged.

OUTLINING RESPONSIBILITIES

There are many ways in which you can define responsibilities – from employment contracts to outcomes for which you are rewarded. While you should appear flexible to your boss, you also need to understand your job, your responsibilities, and your level of authority. You should know what is expected of you in your role and the criteria that will define your success. In turn, you should also understand your boss's responsibilities and the success criteria for his role.

Boss helps define the responsibilities of employee's job

Employee assesses competencies to be achieved based on the job description

BUILDING RAPPORT

You need to create opportunities to encourage an open relationship with your boss that allows both of you to express your feelings. Meet fortnightly to review progress together so that you can both mention any concerns as part of your usual conversation, rather than having to call a special meeting. Listen encouragingly and empathize with your boss, observing how he might be feeling and noticing any recent change in his manner. When rapport is built, it will be easy to share your observations or to ask for your boss's help.

35 Maintain eye contact with your boss and ask open questions.

STANDING AGENDA

---

1. Agree Agenda
   (Listen to each other's suggested agenda items and agree on the three priorities to discuss)

2. Discuss Objective 1

3. Discuss Objective 2

4. Discuss Objective 3

5. Summarize

6. Agree Action Plan

Stick to three objectives per meeting – you can always meet more often

Summarize actions agreed, so that you both leave with the same understanding of what is to be done

◀ **SETTING THE AGENDA**
Reduce any uncertainties at the beginning of a meeting by presenting your items for the agenda and checking what your boss would like to discuss. Agree on the three most important items.

WORKING IN PARTNERSHIP

A good working relationship combines your resources with those of your boss, so that you achieve together more than either of you could have done alone. Your relationship should accommodate individual creativity and initiative. Find out early on how much of your job you will be expected to manage on your own, and how much will be assigned to you by your boss. Your boss may have a different view of the level of autonomy you can exercise on a project over and above the day-to-day administrative tasks associated with your job.

36 Be clear about what your organization expects of you and your boss.

BUILDING TRUST

Trust is built by doing what you say and showing that you can be relied on to deliver agreed outcomes. This process will go through a trial period during which your boss trusts you until proved wrong, or does not trust you until you have proved yourself.

37 Work on reducing barriers to your boss's trust in your abilities.

38 Ask your boss how you are doing and act on her comments.

PROVING YOURSELF

A trusting boss will expect you to deliver what you promised and will only impose restrictions if you let her down. She might be happy if you explain your approach briefly before you go ahead and give progress reports afterwards. A distrusting boss will give you small tests and only let you work unsupervised once you have proved yourself. Plan patiently how you will gain the trust of this kind of boss. Look out for clues that reveal her doubts and work towards resolving them. As trust is built, the brief will be less detailed and the progress reporting less frequent.

Agree on sub-goals that achieve overall goals

Document gives overview of progress

PROGRESS REVIEW CHART

Primary Goal	Reviews
Achieve the Zed project to budget and time.	At least monthly or at each project milestone.
Secondary Goals	**22.09.03** Relocation completed by due date. No complaints about any disruption or lost files.
1. Relocate the filing and library areas without disruption to sales or customer service standards.	
2. Upgrade the central library access area and implement new filing system.	**15.10.03** Upgrade on target for due date. Chasing for delivery of new filing system – ETA one week late.
3. Organize files to be retrieved from relocated area and arranged in new filing system.	**22.10.03** Next review.

Review chart with your boss at key points

Note what went well or not so well

Set date for next review with your boss

◀ **REVIEWING PROGRESS**
Use a Progress Review Chart to give you and your boss an overview of what has been achieved and to identify any problems at an early stage.

39 Update your boss on your latest achievements and learning.

TAKING THE INITIATIVE

It is a challenge to take the initiative yourself, while also acknowledging your boss. Do what you were hired to do and show a responsible approach. This means checking, finishing, and following up your own work. Taking the initiative involves all this and more – it means looking around for what else you can do rather than waiting to be told.

40 Offer to take on extra work to help your overloaded boss.

Team member is surprised to notice a sudden coolness in his boss's usual manner

He thinks back and identifies the cause as an incident in the recent past that his boss had treated lightly at the time

He meets his boss in private, listens to her side of the story, and explains that he did not mean to earn her disapproval

DOS AND DON'TS

✔ Do show your boss that you deliver what you promise.

✔ Do act quickly if your boss feels you have let her down in some way.

✔ Do explain why a job went wrong and ask for help next time.

✘ Don't make excuses that aren't real.

✘ Don't go your own way without ensuring you have your boss's full support.

✘ Don't assume your boss won't notice if something goes wrong.

RETAINING YOUR BOSS'S TRUST

It is important to invest time in maintaining trust between you and your boss. Assess the risks of your boss delegating work to you, and reassure her by explaining how you could control possible risks. If you disagree with your boss, do so in private, unless she asks for your opinion in front of others. If you unintentionally embarrass your boss publicly, apologize immediately. If you sense a misunderstanding, clarify it at a separate meeting. In this way you will minimize the risk of losing your boss's trust when taking the initiative.

◀ REBUILDING TRUST
Trust, once broken, must be rebuilt – however difficult it seems. If you fail to meet your boss's expectations in some way, and feel she has suddenly distanced herself, make sure you have a talk with her and clear up any misunderstanding.

COMPLEMENTING YOUR BOSS'S STYLE

You need to make up for your boss's weaknesses and encourage her to delegate to your strengths, so that you become a complementary team. Focus on your boss's priorities, learn to think like her, and impress her with your forward thinking.

41 Understand your organization's aims and objectives to help your boss.

42 Observe how your boss prioritizes tasks.

43 Read up on major customers and competitors.

UNDERSTANDING YOUR BOSS'S PRIORITIES

Your boss has to achieve organizational objectives. Make sure you know what these are. Ask your boss what her priorities are in achieving these objectives and focus your time on these. If your boss focuses on what she enjoys, rather than what is important to the organization, you need to refocus her attention to ensure that you both spend enough time on the right priorities. Find out the challenges your organization faces and keep abreast of the external competition.

THINKING LIKE THE BOSS

If your boss is short of time and seems to rely on telepathy to communicate, it is important for you to learn to think like her. By understanding her aims and values you can match her thoughts even if you lack her experience or knowledge. Assess whether your boss is a right-brained creative person or a left-brained logical one. By observing how she habitually thinks, you can anticipate her decisions in most situations. If your boss is known for her good judgment, getting to know her decision-making techniques will be invaluable.

QUESTIONS TO ASK YOURSELF

Q When I present a new idea, what does my boss look at first – overview or detail?

Q Does my boss make decisions quickly or put them off?

Q Does my boss resist change or welcome new ideas?

Q Does my boss plan ahead with contingency time, or is she taken by surprise by the unexpected?

KNOWING HOW YOUR BOSS'S MIND WORKS

LEFT BRAIN ANALYZES FACTS

- Is logical
- Thinks in linear steps
- Is analytical
- Needs facts and details
- Observes objectively

RIGHT BRAIN CREATES IDEAS

- Is intuitive
- Thinks laterally
- Views the whole picture
- Admits to feeling emotion
- Allows subjective opinions

SUPPORTING YOUR BOSS

Encourage your boss to acknowledge that you both have strengths and weaknesses, and map out where you can complement each other. Learn how much time your boss needs to make a decision and give timely information. Persuade a resistant boss to make necessary changes, and complete unfinished tasks for an unfocused, chaotic boss. Reassure a boss who is nervous about making decisions by recalling previous successful decisions she made. If she stays in her office, encourage walkabouts, or act as a channel for feedback.

44 Discuss one issue at a time with a single-minded boss.

▼ COMBINING STRENGTHS
If your thinking style is the opposite to that of your boss, maximize your differing strengths and work as a complementary team. The two of you will have a rounded view of any situation and the potential for good combined judgment.

RESERVED COMMUNICATIVE

OBSERVER

CREATIVE

GENERALIST DETAILER

LOGICAL DRIVER

DECISIVE

INDECISIVE

METHODICAL ENERGETIC

MANAGING YOUR WORKLOAD

Your boss will be impressed if you manage your workload efficiently and accomplish important tasks on time. Successful people focus on the right priorities, make optimum use of their time, and do not take on more work than they can handle.

45 Increase the time you allow for tasks if you tend to underestimate.

PRIORITIZING YOUR WORK

Focus on what is important and plan your time realistically, including contingency time for coping with the unexpected. Prioritize your workload – give your most important tasks high priority and delegate as much of your work as you can to leave enough time to meet key deadlines. Bring another priority forward if you complete a task before the deadline.

▼ **ESTIMATING TIME**
Learn to plan your work day efficiently by choosing the best time for different activities. Prioritize the tasks that you have to complete and place them in suitable time slots. Estimate how long each task will take and check the accuracy of your forecast once the jobs are done.

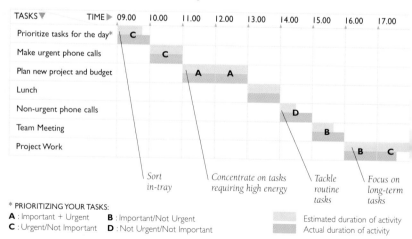

TASKS ▼	TIME ▶	09.00	10.00	11.00	12.00	13.00	14.00	15.00	16.00	17.00
Prioritize tasks for the day*		C								
Make urgent phone calls			C							
Plan new project and budget				A	A					
Lunch										
Non-urgent phone calls							D			
Team Meeting								B		
Project Work									B	C

Sort in-tray

Concentrate on tasks requiring high energy

Tackle routine tasks

Focus on long-term tasks

* PRIORITIZING YOUR TASKS:
A : Important + Urgent **B** : Important/Not Urgent
C : Urgent/Not Important **D** : Not Urgent/Not Important

Estimated duration of activity
Actual duration of activity

REDUCING INTERRUPTIONS

Frequent interruptions prevent you from focusing on important objectives. Analyze your time to check which activities waste time and who disturbs you most, and plan your day to reduce these distractions. You may keep your office door shut at times during the day. If you work in an open-plan office, establish a mutual signal with your colleagues for times when you do not wish to be disturbed. Keep meetings with your boss and colleagues as short as possible, setting a time limit at the beginning to keep the meeting focused. Think about your boss's time management in the same way, and make sure you are not one of his unnecessary "interruptions".

Asks for go-ahead on urgent project

Boss gives immediate approval

MEETING BRIEFLY ▶
It is often a good idea to conduct a brief meeting standing up, as this discourages aimless chatting and makes it easier to leave when you have finished.

---

46 Have your phone calls diverted when you need to concentrate.

47 Explain that you find it difficult, but still say "No" if you need to.

LEARNING TO SAY "NO"

If you have to turn down your boss's request, do so assertively and sensitively. Acknowledge the request and give your reason for being unable to comply. This will usually be because you have a number of other more important priorities that will slip if you take on this extra task. You could outline to your boss all the other tasks you have, so that he can understand your options, and ask what he would do. The best thing is to say "no" as if you mean it – if you try to soften your refusal with excessive apologies or excuses, you will confuse the message. If you are unsure whether you would be able to complete the task, take time to think things through before responding.

SHOWING LOYALTY

Being loyal means supporting and promoting your boss and trying to understand and meet his expectations. Your boss should expect you to be loyal until the moment he takes your loyalty for granted and puts you in an uncomfortable situation.

48 Build two-way relationships with people who are important to you.

49 Check out an organization's values and culture before you join.

50 Speak well of your boss as it reflects well on you.

UNDERSTANDING RECIPROCITY

The relationship between you and your boss is based on fair concessions on each side. Your boss represents the organization that pays you, directs your work to meet objectives, gives you tools to work with, and provides you with job security. You can also expect to be praised for good work, and be given feedback and training. In return, your boss can expect to receive your commitment to producing work at the standard required and your loyalty to the organization. In addition, your boss can expect you to be reliable and to acknowledge his support and guidance.

BEING LOYAL

Loyalty entails making your boss look good in public. By working to increase your boss's credibility, you enhance your own position as well as show loyalty. As long as you share the values of your boss and the organization, loyalty is easy. However, if your boss appears to be doing something that makes you uncomfortable, you should ask him for an explanation. You can then assess whether the difficulty arose because you did not understand the situation fully or if your loyalty is being pushed too far.

Employee outlines her concerns

Boss is able to reassure her

▲ **BEING OPEN**
If your boss's working style seems to go against your principles, voice your discomfort. Your boss's response will help you assess your allegiance to him.

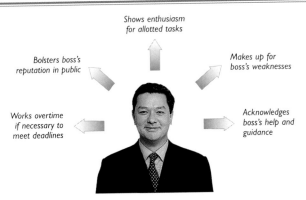

Shows enthusiasm
for allotted tasks

Bolsters boss's
reputation in public

Makes up for
boss's weaknesses

Works overtime
if necessary to
meet deadlines

Acknowledges
boss's help and
guidance

WITHDRAWING LOYALTY

Your loyalty will be tested if your boss is doing something wrong. If he behaves in a way that you disagree with, or that the organization would disapprove of, express your misgivings and give him a chance to change. If the problem continues, you could discuss it with the human resources department. Let your conscience decide how much you can tolerate, but be aware that whistleblowers often pay a personal cost. However, if what your boss is doing is illegal, you may be seen to collude with him if you continue to support him.

▲ **RECOGNIZING LOYALTY**
A loyal employee is committed to his boss and organization. He will stand by his boss until he feels his loyalty is being pushed too far or that the organization will suffer.

51 Be guided by what an objective third party may think.

**GAINING ►
FROM LOYALTY**
An employee remains loyal to his present organization during an interview for a new job. He is rewarded unexpectedly for his discretion.

CASE STUDY

James Kenton was happy in his job and had a good relationship with his boss. However, he was approached by a recruitment agency for a more senior position in an unknown competing company. James was tempted to find out what they would offer but felt loyalty towards his boss and decided to tell her that he had received this offer. His boss's reaction was typically supportive. She told James that she would not like to lose him but did not mind him exploring the new post. James went to the interview and became wary when the headhunter started asking questions about his colleagues. He declined to proceed any further. A few months later his company was taken over by the same competitor and James and his boss were promoted into the new organization. They had checked out his loyalty and discretion beforehand.

SOCIALIZING WITH YOUR BOSS

The difference in status between you and your boss can make socializing difficult to handle. If it is part of your job to socialize with your boss, understand the boundaries of your friendship – or colleagues may resent your relationship.

52 Talk about neutral subjects such as hobbies and holidays.

53 Learn the art of networking from a successful boss.

▼ **REMAINING ALERT**
When socializing with your boss, avoid too much alcohol and stay alert. People may remember what you have said and read more into your words than you meant.

MAKING SMALL TALK

There is an art to making small talk that does not offend anyone and keeps conversation going. In a social situation, chat about topical issues, but avoid controversial subjects. Concentrate on networking, introducing people, and putting everyone at ease, especially if your boss has invited guests. Change the subject if you are asked personal questions, or for sensitive information about your organization.

SOCIALIZING WITH YOUR BOSS

▲ SHARING A SPORT
Enjoying organized out-of-office sporting activities with your boss and colleagues may help to build on the rapport that you share at work.

KEEPING WITHIN BOUNDARIES

The relationship between you and your boss is a business one, and being over-friendly can blur professional and social boundaries. If your boss is also your friend, it may be more difficult to refuse favours, such as being asked to work late frequently. Although you and your boss may believe that you can balance your professional and social relationships, others in the organization may think otherwise. Colleagues might suspect favouritism, and your boss may feel compelled to overcompensate by being harder on you than others. You need to be aware of all these risks.

MAINTAINING THE BALANCE

You may manage to keep a friendship, as well as working relationship with your boss and your colleagues in balance for many years. However, the situation can alter when new people join the organization or if events change in your or your boss's personal life. View the relationship as objectively as possible. Discuss any potential problems with your boss and, if necessary, ask for his help in planning a career move.

CULTURAL DIFFERENCES

In countries such as Sweden, employees and their bosses often socialize within the workplace. Eating together is seen as a natural way to build working relationships. Conversely, in countries with a more formal working culture, such interaction does not take place and bosses tend to eat separately from staff.

DOS AND DON'TS

✔ Do remain professional, however friendly you are with your boss.	✘ Don't forget others' views on your closeness with your boss.
✔ Do support your boss at social gatherings.	✘ Don't make colleagues feel left out.
✔ Do keep in mind organizational policy on friendships at work.	✘ Don't discuss personal details about your boss if the friendship ends.

54 Recognize that relationships may change.

MANAGING CONFLICT

If you ignore conflict, the situation will only get worse.
Take action at the first sign of friction, and learn to deal with
both negative and positive feedback, and harassment or bullying.

RESOLVING CONFLICT

Difficult situations must be handled carefully. Be alert for signs of conflict and analyze what is happening. Keep your own responses in check, while you explore with your boss ways in which you can work together to resolve the problem.

55 Understand how your boss usually reacts and spot changes early.

56 Ensure that your boss regards you as supportive.

57 Note your boss's body language – it is a good indicator of likely conflict.

OBSERVING THE SIGNS

A potential cause of conflict is your manager's insecurity about her position as you gain recognition within the organization. You may be tempted to compete with her but you will achieve more by working with her active co-operation. Look out for signs of any problems, verbal and non-verbal. If your boss seems unusually irritated with you or finds fault with your decision on a minor issue, this could be an early warning signal of impending conflict. Other signs to alert you of an imminent outburst from your boss are foot- or pencil-tapping, and pacing up and down.

THINGS TO DO

1. Act soon if changes in your boss's behaviour worry you.

2. Use "I" statements to tell your boss how you feel.

3. Give your boss a way to save face if she is wrong.

DISCUSSING THE PROBLEM

To discover the root of any conflict, arrange a meeting when you feel your boss is in a calm frame of mind. You may find it daunting to be open with her, but honesty about how you feel is a good starting point. Your boss will probably wish to appear reasonable by hearing you out patiently. Encourage her to bring to the surface any hidden conflict by asking for her feedback.

▼ **RESPONDING WELL**
In some conflict situations, you may need to stand up to your boss. Be assertive rather than aggressive.

Boss is unusually critical of team member's handling of a project at a meeting

Team member responds assertively, giving a quick summary of the progress so far

Team member reacts angrily

Team member gives boss a written report the next day and she is pleased with the way he has dealt with the problem

Boss is displeased at what she sees as disloyal behaviour and their working relationship is damaged

TACKLING THE SITUATION

Review the way in which you and your boss deal with problems. Do you usually shy away from conflict, or do you enjoy it? Avoiding conflict will not resolve problems and hinders your joint effectiveness. A continuous spiral of attack and defence is not helpful either. Define the problem and explain the impact it has on you, without resorting to blame. Listen carefully to your boss's opinions and feelings before summarizing points of agreement and suggestions for action.

RECEIVING FEEDBACK

Feedback on your work can come from your boss, colleagues, and customers, through a formal appraisal, or informally. You need to be able to accept and make use of feedback – whether it is praise or criticism – without it leading to conflict.

58 Make use of feedback to develop and change your role.

59 Be aware of all the responsibilities of your current position.

60 Identify all possible routes for future career growth.

PREPARING FOR APPRAISALS

If you dread appraisals because you have disagreed in the past with the comments made by your boss, change your approach before the next one. View appraisals as an opportunity to help your boss to recognize your successes or to recommend you for promotion. Between appraisals, make notes of all your successful projects rather than try to gather this information just before your appraisal is due. If your boss disagrees with your assessment of your performance, you will have a few examples to illustrate how well you have achieved objectives.

▼ **TAKING STOCK**
Be thorough in your preparation for an appraisal to ensure that you can receive feedback objectively.

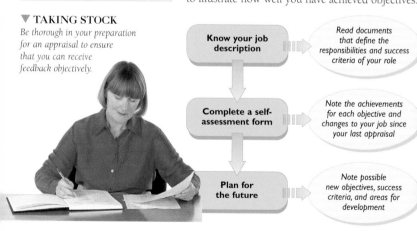

| **Know your job description** | ▶ | Read documents that define the responsibilities and success criteria of your role |

| **Complete a self-assessment form** | ▶ | Note the achievements for each objective and changes to your job since your last appraisal |

| **Plan for the future** | ▶ | Note possible new objectives, success criteria, and areas for development |

ACCEPTING RESPONSIBILITY

If you have not achieved all your objectives, accept responsibility for your own shortcomings, and take steps to improve your performance. If your boss does not give you sufficient feedback, ask him for his views on your work. Learn to handle all his feedback constructively, even if it is given in a demotivating manner. Because you have prepared beforehand, you will be able to evaluate whether or not the feedback is fair.

◀ **COPING WITH NEGATIVE FEEDBACK**
When you receive feedback, even if you do not agree with it, it is important to acknowledge the information about how someone else perceives you and your work, and learn from it.

SETTING OBJECTIVES

Even if you do not always get on with your boss, focusing on SMART objectives will minimize the likelihood of conflict. Have no more than six SMART objectives to focus on. Write out your objectives in specific language, using action words. Describe what you would see, hear, or feel when you have achieved each objective. These qualitative measures, described in your own words, increase your sense of involvement with your job. Achieving objectives will help to keep your commitment high, even if you are in contention with your boss.

61 Set demanding objectives that challenge you.

62 Measure your work both qualitatively and quantitatively.

MEETING SMART OBJECTIVES

SPECIFIC	Establish what you are meant to achieve – and when and how.
MEASURABLE	Define resources to be used and expected results using actual figures.
ACHIEVABLE	Suggest what is achievable and agree on this with your boss.
RELEVANT	Ensure objectives are challenging, yet within your capabilities and control.
TIME-BASED	Agree on the timescale for completion and the frequency of review.

TAKING CRITICISM

If you regard criticism as a means to help you improve, rather than a list of your failings to defend, you will be able to view your boss's feedback objectively and not take it personally. Listen to your boss's comments as if they were observations about someone else. If there is a discrepancy between your own and your boss's view of your performance, you may need to communicate more with your boss. If your boss is reluctant to give you feedback because she fears your reaction, ask her frequently how you can improve. It is better to receive comments about small problems as they arise than to receive all the criticism at once.

ACCEPTING PRAISE

Acknowledge praise from your boss without embarrassment. If you belittle or dismiss praise, you will receive it less often. A simple "thank you" is the best reply if you feel awkward about accepting praise. However, try to find out what exactly your boss appreciated about your work in order to get valuable and focused feedback.

RESPONDING ▶ POSITIVELY

When receiving feedback from your boss, keep your body language open and maintain eye contact. You may agree verbally, but your body language may contradict what you are saying.

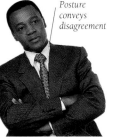

Posture conveys disagreement

Crossed arms show defensiveness

NEGATIVE BODY LANGUAGE

Direct eye contact indicates lack of anything to hide

Body leaning forward shows attentiveness

POSITIVE BODY LANGUAGE

REACTING TO CRITICISM

It is seldom easy to listen to criticism, and your reaction to it depends on the tone of voice and manner in which it is given. In some ways, criticism is even more difficult to take if you accept that it is justified. Give yourself time to think by asking for specifics and taking the time you need to give a considered response:

❝ *I need some time to think about what you said about my work.* ❞

❝ *Which part of the report did you think would be confusing to the customer?* ❞

❝ *What would you like me to change about the way I approach my work?* ❞

EVALUATING CRITICISM

negative feedback comes from a number of
urces, you need to assess the criticism. When
ur boss criticizes you, consider her viewpoint.
her views are too general to act upon, ask for
amples to help you to understand what you
ed to improve. Explore with her when her
pression was formed. Ask for feedback from
ople who work with or for you. In this way,
u can assess common factors that other people,
well as your boss, have noticed, and decide
hat needs to change.

63 Always act
on feedback
from customers.

64 Give less weight
to feedback from
competitors.

65 Take notes during
feedback sessions
to avoid the risk
of ambiguity.

CREATING A PLAN
*ote down actions as they are agreed with
ur boss, with a summary at the end, so
at you leave with a definite plan.*

PLANNING ACTION

Feedback sessions with your boss should result
in action. If the discussion was intended to resolve
an area of conflict, the issue will recur or remain
unresolved if no preventive action is taken. After a
formal appraisal, make an action plan or a
personal development plan and highlight areas to
be focused on, and deadlines by which certain
objectives should be achieved. The plan should
also list the ways in which your boss can help you
to develop the skills you will need.

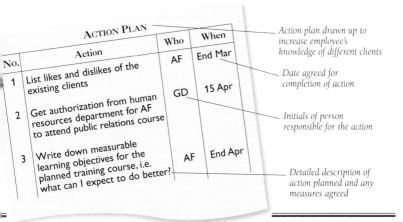

No.	Action	Who	When
1	List likes and dislikes of the existing clients	AF	End Mar
2	Get authorization from human resources department for AF to attend public relations course	GD	15 Apr
3	Write down measurable learning objectives for the planned training course, i.e. what can I expect to do better?	AF	End Apr

Action plan drawn up to increase employee's knowledge of different clients

Date agreed for completion of action

Initials of person responsible for the action

Detailed description of action planned and any measures agreed

TAKING THE INITIATIVE

Showing initiative without usurping your boss's role is a difficult balancing act. Be aware of your boss's reactions to your making decisions or offering suggestions, and acknowledge her help, so that she sees you as a supporter rather than as a competitor.

66 Ask how often your boss wants a review meeting or a report.

QUESTIONS TO ASK YOURSELF

Q Do I know which outcomes are important to my boss?

Q What resources and support can I draw on to achieve the expected results?

Q Do I know what impact the project might have on the organization?

Q Am I aware of any sensitivities or adverse consequences of taking on this work?

CLARIFYING THE BRIEF

Your boss may be happy that you are acting on your own initiative – as long as you reassure her that you are spending your time on the right things. When she briefs you on a new responsibility or project, find out the standards of performance she expects. Some bosses give a scant, rapid brief and you will need to ask questions to make sure you have fully understood what you are to do. Keep your boss informed about progress on key areas to ensure there is no difference of opinion later about what you should have done.

FLOATING SUGGESTIONS

Proposals that conflict with your boss's view may be more acceptable to her if you label them as suggestions. Your boss may not like being told what to do, but suggestions are acceptable since the decision is left open. Before you put forward your idea, outline the reasons behind it. This will tell your boss that she should listen to what you are about to say. If she has to guess at your motives, she may misinterpret your suggestion. If your boss proposes something you disagree with, do not immediately make a counter-suggestion, or she will think that you have not listened. Take the time to consider her views and look for the elements you agree with.

CULTURAL DIFFERENCES

The extent to which you can take the initiative depends on your boss's style, and the organizational culture. In the US, a boss is likely to encourage independent action. In the UK, she will expect polite acknowledgment that she is the boss. In Japan, no step will be taken without the consensus of the whole team.

67 Show enthusiasm for achieving joint objectives.

BUILDING AND SUPPORTING

Always give credit to your boss just as you would expect her to credit you for your own work. In meetings, show your initiative and support for your boss simultaneously by building on what your boss has said or linking your suggestion with her earlier contribution. Never oppose your boss's known point of view in a meeting with others without her knowledge, even if she is not present. Your boss may get to hear of this and may curb your freedom to act on your own.

SHOWING SUPPORT

When your boss is speaking, maintain eye contact and look interested. If your boss is facing opposition, show you agree with your boss and put forward the benefits you see in her suggestions.

Boss outlines plan of action

Team member backs up boss's proposal

Client's initial scepticism about the plan is dispelled

BEING DIPLOMATIC

As you become noticed in the organization, it is diplomatic to remember your boss's help when others are praising you for your achievements. Show your appreciation of your boss's support in your development, without diminishing your own contribution. Even though you may now be approached independently for advice, show respect for your boss – continue to ask rather than tell her what you will do next. Showing due deference while being assertive sends a message to your boss that you understand where your loyalty lies.

68 Be careful of what you say in your boss's absence.

69 Show your boss that you are not in competition.

PROTECTING YOURSELF

It is important to be seen as someone who delivers as promised, to avoid being blamed when things go wrong. What your boss needs during challenging times is not conflict but someone he can trust to handle important issues with no unpleasant surprises.

> **70** Ensure that you and your boss present a united front in a crisis.

> **71** Drop, delay, or delegate anything that is not urgent if you sense a crisis is imminent.

KEEPING THE RIGHT FOCUS

When things go wrong in organizations, people tend to look for a scapegoat, and you need to protect your reputation if you want to stay in your job. In a crisis, you and your boss may come under scrutiny, and it is essential to remain focused on what is important. Review your key aims. Often, 20 per cent of your effort achieves 80 per cent of the results – find out which objectives have the maximum effect. Then consider the publicity factor – which goals most enhance your and your boss's reputation if you succeed, or cause most embarrassment if you fail? Focus on these few key objectives to accelerate your impact on results.

> **72** Shut out any distractions in times of difficulty.

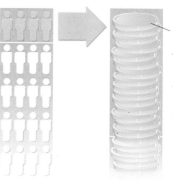

Over 80 per cent of revenue comes from under 20 per cent of customers, so your main focus should be that small proportion of customers

USING THE 80/20 RULE ▶
The 80/20 rule devised by Vilfredo Pareto states that a few causes are responsible for a large percentage of the effect. This can be applied to any number of situations – for example, to identify your key customers and prioritize your tasks accordingly.

BEING SEEN TO DELIVER

It is not enough to perform your job to a high standard if you and your boss are under threat. You should ensure that other people are aware of your success as a team. It is too late to have a publicity campaign when the downturn has started. You need to be working on this during the good times. Manage your own and your boss's chances of survival by focusing on your influential internal customers as well as external ones.

73 Pre-empt problems with other people by sustaining good relationships.

▼ **AVOIDING SURPRISES**
Ensure that your boss and clients are never caught unawares by adverse information. Advise them of the problem before someone else does.

GUARDING AGAINST THE UNEXPECTED

In a fast-moving business environment, there is always a risk that unforeseen problems will arise. Even if your boss trusts you to use your initiative and make decisions, keep him well-briefed – especially about anything unexpected. Anticipate conflicts that might arise with customers or colleagues in other departments. Guard against mistakes that you can avoid. Own up to more major problems, with proposed solutions, in time for them to be corrected.

Team member puts forward a plan to tackle a potential problem

Boss is reassured that the clients' interests are being protected

DEALING WITH STRESS

Stress is often a sign of potential conflict that has not been dealt with. Being able to identify symptoms of stress in yourself or your boss will enable you to do something about the causes before stress becomes a problem that affects your work.

74 Talk over stressful situations with a friend before you talk to your boss.

75 Take relaxation breaks to relieve work pressure.

76 Spot the physical signs of unresolved emotional conflict.

RECOGNIZING SYMPTOMS

Being constantly late, forgetful, unable to make decisions, and unconcerned about personal appearance are behavioural symptoms of stress. Emotional symptoms include anger or fearfulness, and can lead to a withdrawal from relationships at work. The physical effects of stress, such as back or neck pain, or ulcers, often recur. Although all these could be due to unrelated problems, when you notice a number of symptoms simultaneously in yourself or your boss, stress is the likely cause.

IDENTIFYING CAUSES

Conflict in the workplace can cause stress and high levels of stress can cause conflict. Your boss may expect too much from you, leading to a deterioration in your relationship and the quality of your work. Or she may not allow you any control over schedules, or a say in decision-making – feeling undervalued and underused can prove to be equally stressful. If you feel that stress is affecting your performance and you are losing your perspective, raise the issue with your boss before the situation overwhelms you.

Team member is exhausted as she frequently has to work overtime

▲ **WORKING LATE**
Unpredictable working hours are a major cause of stress. Organize your tasks and your time to avoid having to work overtime continually.

MANAGING STRESS

If you feel constantly under pressure at work, you need to review how you manage and delegate work. You can do the same for your boss and make suggestions about how you could support, or be supported, to keep both of you as tension-free as possible. Long-term stress has an adverse effect on creativity, health, and performance, and all these can affect the profitability of an organization. Exercise regularly, adopt a well-balanced diet and eat at regular times, and get enough sleep to give yourself a chance to cope – even thrive – under pressure. Encourage your boss to maintain the same regime.

77 Recognize that you need some short-term stress to raise performance and tackle challenges.

▼ BALANCING WORK AND LIFE

Planning focuses your time on important goals. If you have a disorganized working style, you will spend this time reacting to crises rather than concentrating on your priorities.

▼ GETTING AWAY

When you are spending time with your family or friends, leave all work issues behind you. Your time off should rejuvenate you to face your routine tasks again.

BALANCED LIFE

Activities are planned and time is saved

40%

35%

5%   12%   13%

UNBALANCED LIFE

More time is spent at work since activities are unplanned

50%   30%

7%   6%   7%

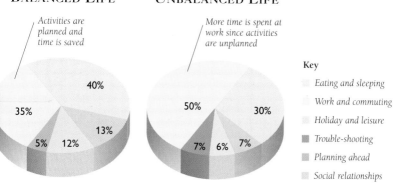

Key

▨ Eating and sleeping

▨ Work and commuting

▨ Holiday and leisure

■ Trouble-shooting

■ Planning ahead

▨ Social relationships

COPING WITH HARASSMENT

*O*ne of the most damaging forms of
conflict at work can be harassment
from your boss. In such a situation you need
to state what you find unacceptable. If
nothing changes, know your rights and how
to protect yourself if you decide to complain.

78 Ask questions to ascertain if your boss's harassment is deliberate.

ASSERTIVE BILL OF RIGHTS

I have the right to:
- Be treated with respect
- Express my opinions and feelings
- Have my contribution listened to
- Ask for what I want and need
- Express my beliefs
- Say "no" without feeling guilty
- Make mistakes as part of gaining experience
- Choose how I behave and take the consequences
- Receive reasonable notice of changes to my job
- Work in an environment that is not damaging to me

KNOWING YOUR RIGHTS

If you are being harassed by your boss, as a one-off incident or by being worn down over time through unkind or prejudiced comments, you have rights. In a one-to-one meeting, tell your boss how you feel about his behaviour. If he is sexually harassing you or making offensive racial remarks, tell him to stop. If you are being treated unfairly, remember there are employment laws against discrimination in the workplace, and human rights laws to preserve your dignity at work.

◀ **SETTING THE LIMITS**
Remembering these guidelines will help you realize when your boss has overstepped the boundaries. These rights bring with them the responsibility to afford the same rights to others.

PREPARING YOUR CASE

If your boss's behaviour is upsetting you, keep a diary of events and prepare to present your case to someone else for help. Record the date and time of every incident, anyone else observing or involved, and what action you took. Keep copies of any correspondence or notes of relevant conversations. Prepare to follow the grievance procedure of your organization – this will entail making a complaint in writing to senior management and may also involve the human resources department.

79 Assess the impact of your boss's behaviour on you.

80 Ensure you have a network of people to support you.

81 Look up your organization's policy on bullying and harassment.

TAKING ACTION

If, having spoken to your boss, the unacceptable behaviour continues, approach someone else. Take outside advice, if this is free of charge, before you ask for internal help. Talk in confidence to unions, government-funded or other agencies, or lawyers, who advise citizens on their legal rights and can help you with your case. If an assault is involved or you are forced to leave your job unfairly, this could involve legal action. Accept help to cope with the likely consequences, both legal and emotional.

DECIDING TO LEAVE

A bullying boss can erode your self-esteem, attack your self-confidence, and leave you afraid of the next humiliating experience. You have to decide whether the job is worth the personal costs. Consider if there is any future for the working relationship. Support within the organization from colleagues, personnel, or senior management can alleviate the situation. If you do not receive inside support, you may have no choice but to leave.

▲ **SEEKING LEGAL HELP**
Take legal advice before resigning, to find out if you are eligible for compensation for constructive dismissal.

STANDING ▶ YOUR GROUND
Sally got used to her boss's criticism and blamed herself instead of insisting her boss treat her fairly. Help from a colleague, her follow-up action, and her boss's change of behaviour, saved her from further psychological suffering. Her boss was also spared from legal action for harassment and bullying.

CASE STUDY

Nothing Sally did was ever good enough for her boss. When Sally asked what she could do to improve her work, he would dismissively say that he had no time to go through her long list of mistakes. Gradually Sally lost confidence and spent many unproductive hours trying to correct her work on her own. A new employee joined work and he was much more assertive with the boss. He told Sally their boss had no right to cause her such distress and suggested she ask him for specific feedback. In a meeting, with her boss, Sally stated how upset she was that her work was not valued and described how she felt their relationship could be improved. Her boss was surprised by the feedback and apologized for being impatient under stress. Over time he realized he could rely on his team for effective help without bullying them.

IMPROVING YOUR PROSPECTS

Your boss can help you gain the skills you need to achieve a better salary package and promotion. Take on more responsibility in your job and gain your boss's agreement to your career plans.

EXPANDING YOUR ROLE

It would be surprising if your role at work remained unchanged between annual reviews. There will always be new aspects of your job with potential for growth and gaining experience. It is up to you to make the best of these opportunities.

82 Recall a challenge you have overcome and use it to learn about yourself.

83 Record what has changed in your role and why.

POINTS TO REMEMBER

- The success of long-term goals should be periodically assessed.
- The latest professional trends need to be kept in mind.
- Self-development should not be neglected or postponed.

REVIEWING YOURSELF

Your appraisal is a formal opportunity to review, with your boss, the changes in your role, and to record these as a revised job description. However you should also review your own progress independently of your boss and update your CV at least once a year. Reflect on the new skills you have acquired and strengths you have shown. Identify aspects of your performance that could improve. Note the changes over the last year and anticipate the likely changes in the next year. Continuous improvement is essential in any role – if nothing has changed, you have a problem.

FOCUSING ON AREAS OF GROWTH

By reflecting on what has changed in your role, you can focus on areas for development in discussions with your boss. Any expansion of your organization is your best chance for proving yourself. Ask your boss questions about any new initiatives the organization may be planning. Do some research on whether outside trends favour the changes proposed. Ask yourself what impact the new direction will have on your future role. If you see a real opportunity for growth in a new area, volunteer, with your boss's support, to work on associated projects to get yourself noticed.

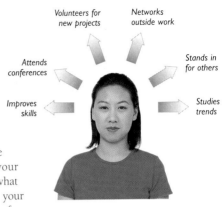

Volunteers for new projects

Networks outside work

Attends conferences

Stands in for others

Improves skills

Studies trends

▲ **EXPANDING HORIZONS**
It is essential to capitalize on as many growth opportunities as possible, within and outside the organization, to expand your role.

GAINING EXPERIENCE

In a flat organizational structure, promotion could be slower than you would like. Discuss with your boss how to gain the experience and skills you will need to be promoted. For example, could you do this through special projects, secondments to another area or an associated organization, or by standing in for someone in a more senior position while they are away? As you build trust with your boss, you can persuade her to delegate more and more responsibility to you. Deputizing for her when she is away becomes a natural next step. Offer to attend conferences and report back to colleagues on what you have learned that will be useful to the organization.

◀ **MAKING THE MOST OF CONTACTS**
In your own time, network with people involved in some way with your work. Build up a contact list of people who can keep you updated on professional developments or who may become customers in the future.

LEADING FROM BEHIND

If your boss's performance is standing still, you are both going backwards in real terms. Show leadership by continuously improving your own and your boss's skills and supporting your boss while at the same time retaining visibility yourself.

84 Help your boss recognize that change is taking place at work.

85 Link suggestions for improvement with profitability.

86 Look for suitable mentors for you and your boss.

SUGGESTING CHANGES

In a learning organization, suggesting new ways to do things is a natural way of life. Review performance improvements you have observed with your boss and the benefits to the organization in terms of business objectives achieved. Your suggestions will be more acceptable if you link improvements to the increased satisfaction of customers, employees, and shareholders. Other relevant objectives might be revenue increases, cost and time savings, and avoiding waste.

▼ **LEARNING TO GROW**
A learning organization is constantly looking for ways in which it can develop and improve its performance.

All participate in decision-making

Information is widely shared

Feedback encourages development

Plans adapted to new knowledge

Everyone contributes ideas

Team reflects on what they have learned

87 Suggest hiring research students to inject new ideas.

DEVELOPING YOUR BOSS

Your boss may have amassed experience over the years but, like everyone, she needs to continuously improve and keep her knowledge updated. As you discuss your development with your boss, you can encourage her to consider appropriate activities for herself. If you have discovered interesting network groups, introduce your boss to your contacts or, with her permission, suggest her as a conference speaker. Keep her abreast of research or information on other organizations relevant to new initiatives she is working on.

▼ **HELPING YOUR BOSS KEEP UP TO DATE**
Encourage your boss to attend meetings on relevant topics arranged by membership organizations for managers and directors to gather ideas to try out at work.

Manager contributes an idea for networking group to improve sales

Senior manager explains how she achieves results

New manager jots down key learning points

RETAINING VISIBILITY

To lead from behind successfully, you will have to resign yourself to your boss gaining glory from your joint achievements. A fair boss will tell others about your contribution. In informal conversation, assess how visible you are to other departments or senior management. Put your name on reports you write and observe whether your boss leaves this information on copies sent to others. Suggest ways in which you can represent your organization to retain visibility without antagonizing your boss.

THINGS TO DO

1. Check informally if others know of your contribution.
2. Include the names of those responsible for new ideas in minutes of meetings.
3. Participate in networking or action groups.

FINDING HELP WITH SELF-DEVELOPMENT

Identify your development needs and suggest to your boss the activities and training that will help you most. You can persuade your boss to invest in your future and make yourself more marketable by presenting the benefits for both of you.

88 Think long term if you wish to progress higher in the organization.

89 Manage yourself first to have time to manage others well.

IDENTIFYING YOUR NEEDS

Look at your present performance and the skills you might need in a future job to identify areas for development. Ask your boss what skills she thinks are needed for a job at the next level. As you rise higher, you will be judged on your people skills and how effectively you manage resources. How well do you manage people? Can you set up and lead teams? How adept are you at long-term strategic thinking – an essential skill if you want to progress higher in the organization?

CASE STUDY
Pablo Garcia had received feedback in his appraisal that his interpersonal skills needed to be developed. As suggested, he attended a workshop on communication skills. During the training, Pablo watched a video recording of himself talking with a colleague and was able to observe that his body language conveyed the opposite of enthusiasm.
At the next team meeting, when Pablo had to present a new idea to the team, he made a point of maintaining eye contact with the whole team and varying the tone of his voice. He then asked questions to gain feedback and looked interested in the team's reaction. Impressed by the clear presentation, his colleagues supported his ideas for the new project. Seeing his success at winning the team over, his boss congratulated him and made a mental note to put his name forward for a promotion.

◀ WORKING ON YOUR WEAKNESSES
In this example, an employee made full use of a self-development course to earn praise from his boss and colleagues, and improve his chances of promotion.

UNDERSTANDING THE THREE TYPES OF TRAINING

PRINCIPLES	PEOPLE	PROCESSES
● Business Management	● Career Counselling	● Critical Thinking
● Finance	● Coaching	● Problem-solving
● Health & Safety	● Delegation	● Process Management
● Marketing	● Facilitation	● Project Management
● Selling	● Leadership	● Strategic Management
● Technical or Technological	● Recruitment & Selection	● Time Management

PLANNING DEVELOPMENT ACTIVITIES

Work out with your boss the optimum timing and type of development activities to meet your needs. There are many ways, in addition to formal courses, to achieve personal growth. Set yourself a target of reading two management books per month on the areas you need to develop. Play tapes on management topics while you commute. Ask your boss to hire management videos that employees can watch at lunchtime. Note the key points you have learned, and put them into practice.

90 Listen to audio tapes or CDs of self-help books.

91 Think laterally about how to gain self-development.

▲ LEARNING TOGETHER
Meet up with colleagues occasionally to share the self-development techniques you have learned, and try to make them part of your routine.

LOOKING AHEAD

Reassure your boss that your organization will gain a return for the expense incurred by it on your self-development. A lengthy course at a business school, for example, is a large investment by any employer. Your organization may insist that you remain an employee for some time beyond course completion, so that you can apply your newly gained skills to your work. Apart from relying on your employer, find ways to undertake self-development in your own time, to improve your prospects for promotion.

GAINING AGREEMENT

If you want your boss to agree to something you propose, choose your moment carefully. Present the benefits well – especially if you are requesting a promotion or transfer, or an investment in your development – to make it easy for him to say "yes".

92 Check your boss's schedule to ensure he can give you his full attention.

QUESTIONS TO ASK YOURSELF

Q Is my proposal concise and easy to assimilate?

Q Is my case convincing as a business proposition?

Q At what time of the day does my boss function best?

Q Is my boss under particular pressure from some other work at the moment?

Q Is my boss expressing real concerns I need to reassure him about, or just excuses?

CHOOSING YOUR MOMENT

Be sensitive to times when your boss is under pressure, but do not put off important issues indefinitely. If your boss agrees with your proposal, you will probably get an immediate response. Delay usually means there was something wrong with your proposal, unless your boss has been out of the office or is occupied on a particular project. Note your boss's designated times for going through his in-tray, making phone calls, or when his open door indicates that you can interrupt. Observe whether he prefers to meet team members early in the morning or later in the day.

Employee has adequate time to explain her plan clearly

▼ TIMING IT RIGHT
Choose the time when your boss is most receptive if you want an affirmative response to your proposal.

PRESENTING THE BENEFITS

Think of the benefits of your proposal from your boss's perspective – as an individual, leader of your team, and as a representative of the organization. A boss with a financial background will want to make sure you have prepared a realistic and cost-conscious budget for your proposal. If your boss is a people person, your benefits should relate to satisfaction, motivation, and teamwork. Describe how your performance will improve, if your proposal is accepted, in terms that match your boss's way of thinking.

93 List the benefits of your proposal succinctly.

94 Review all the factors that will affect your plan

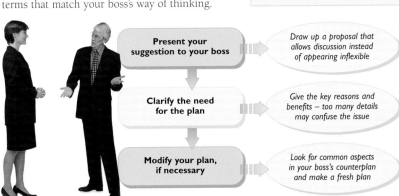

Present your suggestion to your boss
Draw up a proposal that allows discussion instead of appearing inflexible

Clarify the need for the plan
Give the key reasons and benefits – too many details may confuse the issue

Modify your plan, if necessary
Look for common aspects in your boss's counterplan and make a fresh plan

▲ **PREPARING A FLEXIBLE PLAN**
Do your research well before you present your plan so that you can counter your boss's objections, or make adjustments to your plan where necessary.

95 Ask questions to assess your boss's reaction to your proposed plan.

MAKING "YES" THE EASY OPTION

Present a well-thought-out, logical plan and make it hard for your boss to refuse. If your boss hesitates to give his approval, keep questioning him until you understand his reservations. Make sure these are legitimate concerns rather than delaying tactics. Attempt to overcome your boss's concerns by presenting the benefits and ask for his agreement. If at this point you still receive a negative reply, ask what it is that is still not quite right. Persistence should pay off in the end.

NEGOTIATING A RISE

*M*ost people will accept a salary that is not the highest available for the job, as long as the amount feels fair as an indication of their worth. Assess your value to the organization and present a case for a rise, based on the value you have added.

96 Make your case for a rise factually, assertively, and persistently.

Employee asks for pay rise in an open and confident manner

Boss listens attentively

▲ **BEING SURE OF YOUR WORTH**

Asking your boss for a rise does not imply disloyalty to him. Overcome such misconceptions by confidently presenting your arguments for a higher salary.

VALUING YOURSELF

You may feel uncomfortable asking your boss for more money. However, if you think that you are no longer receiving the appropriate pay for the job you are doing, you need to ask for a rise to show that you value yourself. You may be the type of person who focuses on doing a good job and would be happy to take a promotion based on job title rather than money – but you need to make sure you are not being taken for granted. Research salaries for the same kind of job in your own or another organization to ensure that you are proposing a fair salary, before you approach your boss.

DOS AND DON'TS

✔ Do be sure of your major objective.	✘ Don't lose focus on your key objective.
✔ Do outline the elements of your package that you would like to improve.	✘ Don't be so swayed by your boss's point of view that you fail to present your case well.
✔ Do concede on the items of least importance to you.	✘ Don't concede to your boss's modifications straightaway.
✔ Do confirm what was agreed upon.	✘ Don't get emotional if you are turned down.
✔ Do present options so your boss has a choice.	✘ Don't present a case unsupported by facts.

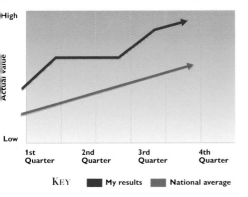

▲ TOTALLING UP THE BALANCE

Prepare a record of your successes. Put an actual value, such as revenue generated or number of hours saved, against each entry to convince your boss that you deserve a pay rise.

SHOWING HOW YOU ADD VALUE

If you focus on your personal needs when you ask for a rise, you are unlikely to meet with a positive response. Present a good case based on the extra responsibilities that you have taken on, money that you have saved or earned for your organization, or additional skills you are applying to save time and improve quality. Drawing up a value-added business case is most likely to gain the consideration of your boss.

Find out the market rate for similar jobs	Make a list of your achievements	Ask for a rise armed with facts and figures

MAKING IT HAPPEN

When you are convinced about your added-value business case, ask your boss for a one-to-one meeting. Calm, persistent repetition of your request is the right approach. If your boss raises objections, explain why you think the salary range you are asking for is right. If your boss thinks you do not deserve a pay rise, despite your business case, ask him what else you would need to do. If your boss tells you that his hands are tied as he has budget constraints, the minimum you should ask for is a review within six months. Follow up this discussion with a memo mentioning the date agreed upon and thanking him – it will be useful to refer to later if he needs reminding of his promise.

▲ BEING PREPARED

You can confidently ask your boss for a rise if you do your research well and have all the relevant information in place.

POINTS TO REMEMBER

- You need to believe in your own worth and in the value you add to the organization.

- An increase in your salary will often entail an increase in responsibilities or workload.

- The benefits of what you suggest should be outlined to your boss.

- Your boss should be made aware of your achievements.

ACHIEVING PROMOTION

Your boss has a direct influence on your chances of promotion. Make it clear to her that you are ready for promotion by behaving as if you are already at the next level. She may even offer help on external promotion if you have been open with her.

97 Always advise your boss before you apply for internal promotion.

98 Keep your boss updated about your career goals.

99 Tell your boss when you feel ready for promotion.

MANAGING YOUR PROMOTION

Your organization's appraisal scheme may require your boss to discuss career paths with you. Review your opportunities for internal promotion with your boss at appraisal time and ask her to help in facilitating the transition. If you plan to apply within the organization, discuss it with your boss first. She will be a key referee for both internal and external applications. Assess the new skills you have acquired with her and review how they will help in your transfer to your new position.

BEHAVING AS IF PROMOTED

If your boss is a good role-model, you should already be clear on how to behave at the next level. Observe who is valued in your workplace and for what skills and personal qualities. If working long hours appears to be the common factor for being promoted, consider if this is what you really want. Initiative, creativity, or good people skills may be the criteria you need to emulate. Network with people who could be useful when you are promoted.

Friendly contact gives tips on job

GAINING THE SUPPORT OF OTHERS ▶
Do not worry about taking up the time of people who could help you up the career ladder. Turn your boss and colleagues into advocates for you.

BE READY
With your people skills in place, you are ready for a more responsible role.

◀ **TRANSFERRING SKILLS**
Take advantage of every opportunity to polish your skills to make the transition to a higher-level job smooth and trouble-free.

INTERACT WITH YOUR BOSS
Use listening and questioning skills to learn from your boss.

HELP OTHERS
Develop your management skills by investing time in the talents of those who work with you.

Makes use of transferable skills to climb the corporate ladder

MANAGE INDIRECTLY
Recognize the larger team that you work with outside your work group and use your influencing skills.

START NOW
Even if you do not have a large team to practise on, you can start working on developing the leadership skills that you need for your future promotion.

HONING YOUR SKILLS

Listen carefully to feedback about the competencies needed for a promotion – from your boss and others whose opinion you value – and start working on them. Your time and resource management talents and leadership skills need to match the level above you. Count how many relationships with colleagues, contractors, and suppliers you have to manage. You probably have influence over a larger number of people than you directly manage. One way to improve your management skills is to volunteer as a mentor to others.

POINTS TO REMEMBER

● Your behaviour should match that of people at the next level.
● You may sometimes need to make it clear to your boss that you are ready for promotion.
● It is important to discuss your career goals in general terms with contacts outside the office.
● You need to ask your boss how to be selected for promotion and make a good start in the new role.

63

PREPARING FOR CHANGE

Find out who has been successfully promoted in the organization and note any common factors. Ask what was most difficult and most easy about the transition. If your boss supports your case for promotion, ask her whether she agrees with your assessment of how you meet the criteria for the new job. Recognize her contribution to your readiness for promotion and consider how you could minimize disruption when you move on. Think about how you could help your boss in finding a successor.

THINGS TO DO

1. Ask your boss what qualities you need to be promoted to her level.

2. Ask her how she would deal with issues in the new job.

3. See if any of your team members can be promoted to take your place.

Well-prepared candidate faces panel with confidence

BEING INTERVIEWED

Try to find out who else is competing for the promotion. Assess their strengths and weaknesses and look at the same for yourself. Never assume that the interviewer will know about your past achievements, whether you are an internal or external candidate. This is not the time to be modest – you need to state what your strengths are and cite successful projects.

◀ **HANDLING INTERVIEWS**
Be prepared for a one-to-one interview, a panel interview, group sessions, or an interview at an assessment centre for the selection process.

KNOWING THE LIKELY QUESTIONS

WHAT YOU ASK	WHAT YOU ARE ASKED
● What major challenges do you anticipate in the next year?	● What has presented the greatest challenge to you in the last two years?
● What are the key success factors in this job?	● What are your strengths and what are you least confident about?
● What qualities are you looking for in the person who does this job?	● What has been the most valuable thing you have learned in your current job?
● If I am offered this job is there anything in particular I could do to prepare for it?	● Why should we offer you this job?

PLANNING FOR SUCCESS

You should devise an outline plan for what you would do in your first few months of the new job. You may be asked about this at your interview to see if you have really understood what is involved. Talk to your boss and anyone who knows the new department or organization you are joining. Read any relevant reports, articles, or publicity. Find out what your predecessor was like, how much of a change you will be to your new team, and how are they performing currently. Assess who will be your new allies. If you can, plan to take a holiday before starting your new job. Use this time to relax and also to think through exactly how you will make a good impression with your new team, your new colleagues, and your new boss.

100 Prepare your own questions to ask at interviews.

101 Set yourself new and challenging goals to achieve in your new job.

▼ **CELEBRATING SUCCESS**
Celebrate your hard-earned promotion with all those who have been instrumental, directly or indirectly, in the achievement.

ASSESSING YOUR ABILITY

Test how well you are able to manage your boss and whether you have succeeded in turning your boss into your greatest advocate. Answer the following questions honestly. If your answer is 'Never' mark option 1; if it is 'Always' mark option 4 and so on. Add your scores together, and refer to the analysis at the end to see how you have scored. Use your answers to identify areas that need improvement.

OPTIONS	
1	Never
2	Occasionally
3	Frequently
4	Always

1 I plan my future career development with my goals and priorities in mind.

| 1 | 2 | 3 | 4 |

2 I treat my boss in the same way as I would treat a key customer.

| 1 | 2 | 3 | 4 |

3 I am aware of my own strengths and weaknesses.

| 1 | 2 | 3 | 4 |

4 I encourage my boss to pass on knowledge and experience to me.

| 1 | 2 | 3 | 4 |

5 I have a clear idea of what is important to me in my life.

| 1 | 2 | 3 | 4 |

6 I make it a point to discuss shared values with my boss.

| 1 | 2 | 3 | 4 |

7 I set objectives for what I wish for in different areas of my life.

1 2 3 4

8 I observe how people think in different ways.

1 2 3 4

9 I manage my work-life balance in my day-to-day routine.

1 2 3 4

10 I am able to say "No" assertively when necessary.

1 2 3 4

11 I encourage my boss and colleagues to give me feedback.

1 2 3 4

12 I keep my boss updated on the progress of projects I am working on.

1 2 3 4

13 I observe and assess my boss's strengths and weaknesses.

1 2 3 4

14 I make sure that I understand exactly what is expected of me.

1 2 3 4

15 I am assertive with my boss rather than passive or aggressive.

1 2 3 4

16 I encourage my boss to delegate responsibility and authority to me.

1 2 3 4

17 I listen carefully to my boss to identify any potential problems.

1 2 3 4

18 I review my workload and discuss priorities with my boss.

1 2 3 4

19 I give my boss positive feedback about our achievements.

1 2 3 4

20 I make suggestions for change that my boss is happy to accept.

1 2 3 4

21 I pick the best time to discuss difficult issues with my boss.

1 2 3 4

22 I know how to create a good impression with my boss.

1 2 3 4

23 I present my boss with solutions, not problems.

1 2 3 4

24 I make sure my boss knows about any problems before anyone else.

1 2 3 4

25 I give constructive feedback on my boss's working style.

1 2 3 4

26 I present information in the way my boss prefers.

1 2 3 4

27 I ask open questions and maintain eye contact while talking with my boss.

| 1 | 2 | 3 | 4 |

28 I deliver over and above the expectations of my boss.

| 1 | 2 | 3 | 4 |

29 I am flexible, but I also know when to stand my ground.

| 1 | 2 | 3 | 4 |

30 I am loyal to my boss and support my boss's actions and ideas.

| 1 | 2 | 3 | 4 |

31 I summarize actions agreed upon with my boss.

| 1 | 2 | 3 | 4 |

32 I ensure that my boss is aware that I add value to my job.

| 1 | 2 | 3 | 4 |

ANALYSIS

Now that you have completed the self-assessment, add up your total score and check your performance. Whatever level of success you have achieved, there is always room for further development. Identify your weakest areas, then refer back to the relevant sections of this book.

32–63: You need to be more proactive in managing your boss. Try to understand your boss's style of working. Be clear on objectives before you discuss them.

64–95: You are largely aware of how to manage your boss. Practise being more assertive and identify areas for self-development.

96–128: You are adept at managing your boss. Continuously develop yourself by asking for feedback and reviewing what you have learned.

69

INDEX

ACKNOWLEDGMENTS

AUTHOR'S ACKNOWLEDGMENTS

The production of this book has called on the skills of a great many people and I would like to thank them all for their excellent teamwork. I am particularly grateful to Adèle Hayward and Nicky Munro, whose enthusiasm and insightful comments have been an inspiration.

PUBLISHER'S ACKNOWLEDGMENTS

Dorling Kindersley would like to thank the following for their help and participation in producing this book:

Picture research Kavita Dutta
Picture librarian Richard Dabb
Indexer Margaret McCormack
Photography Gary Ombler, Steve Gorton, Matthew Ward, Andy Crawford, Tim Ridley

PICTURE CREDITS

Key: *a* above, *b* bottom, *c* centre, *l* left, *r* right, *t* top
Corbis: Tom Stewart 4c; Jon Feingersh 7; Yang Liu 36; Michael Keller 49; Darama 53bl and 65; Raoul Minsart 57.
Stone/Getty Images: 48tl; **Superstock:** 21bl

All other images © Dorling Kindersley.
For further information see www.dkimages.com

AUTHOR'S BIOGRAPHY

Christina Osborne is Chief Executive of the strategic human resources consultancy Business Solutions, www.BSol.co.uk. Christina advises clients, ranging from entrepreneurs to multinationals, on designing organizations and developing people to succeed. Her roles as executive director have spanned personnel, marketing, and strategic planning, including mergers and acquisitions. Christina has held non-executive board roles in both public and private sectors and been engaged as a speaker on human resource strategy and as a mentor to chief executives and directors leading organizational change. Her wealth of experience on organizational strategy has confirmed the importance of executives learning how to manage their boss, especially in times of change. Christina is a Fellow of both the Chartered Institute of Personnel and Development and the Chartered Institute of Directors. She is author of *Appraising Staff* and *Dealing with Difficult People* in the Essential Managers series.